The Ski

We put on our jackets and hats.
We put on our goggles and mittens.
We put on our sunscreen.

We put on our boots.
We put on our skis.
We are ready
for our ski lesson.

Our ski instructor meets us at the bunny hill.
Her name is Gaby.

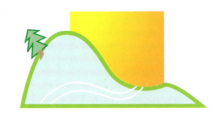

We take our skis on and off.
We walk in the snow.

We walk uphill sideways.
Gaby calls this sidestepping.

We walk uphill in big Vs.
Gaby calls this herringbone.

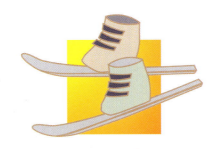

We catch the rope tow.
Gaby calls this
the carrot ride.
It pulls us up the hill.

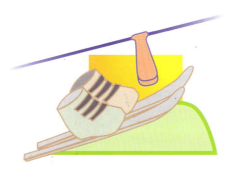

13

We get in a line.
Gaby goes first.

We make a wedge
with our skis.
Gaby calls this pizza pie.

We make our skis go straight.
Gaby calls this french fries.

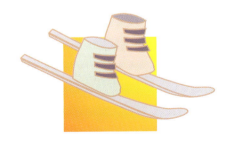

We make turns.
We ski around cones.

We make little jumps.

We fall down.
We laugh a lot.

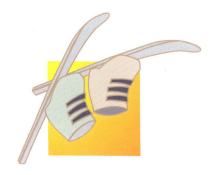

Our lesson is over.
"See you later," we say.